To Lisa, and Earl.

Thankyou both for your friendship and support.

This is the very first book I have ever signed and I am so happy that it is for you.

The warmest of best wishes.

WINDSWEPT

POEMS OF LOVE

BY OWAIN GLYN

Outer Banks Publishing Group
Outer Banks/Raleigh USA

FIRST EDITION
ISBN 10 - 0990679020
ISBN 13 – 978-0-9906790-2-8
eISBN: 978-1311996626

Published September 2015

ACKNOWLEDGEMENTS

I would like to recognize Mary L. Tabor for her support and assistance.

WHAT READERS ARE SAYING...

Welsh writer Owain Glyn has brought us a collection of poetry worthy of his homeland. Windswept is exquisite, you will want to keep it by your bedside for years to come. - V L Sloan

Owain Glyn's Windswept brings to mind the great romantic poetry of the nineteenth century. Its nuances eloquently displayed through the shifting winds that have swept through the heart of this wonderful poet. - Lisa Cole-Allen.

Windswept is awash with words that appear simple but work like magic. This is poetry that Tom, Dick and Harriet (and I) can read, and enjoy. It connects with us, and has the power to transform us. - Colm Herron

Table of Contents

WINDSWEPT DISCOVERY

Senses

When you place your hand, in mine,
I lose all sense,
Of space,
And time.
I feel sweet electricity,
Which flows
And courses,
All through me.

And when I gaze into your eyes,
For me, it comes,
As no surprise.
That I am lost,
I'm all at sea,
You navigate,
Each port for me,
You guide me, ever carefully.

When I hear your soft, sweet voice,
It's just as if,
I have no choice.
I can,
But trust,
The melody,

That touches,
And caresses me.

All I am,
All that I'll be,
All the very best in me.
Rests within,
Your very soul,
Without you, love,
I am not whole.

The Wonder of Words

We agreed to meet
And speak.
For weeks before
I planned what I should say
On this momentous day
And make a start
To win your heart.
I wandered through
The poets' muse
To choose
A suitable romantic phrase
To daze

And amaze.
But
Instead of many hued confetti
My words
Tumbled out
Like cold, confused
Spaghetti!
My tongue was tied
I tried
To recover
Alas, with no success
It was a mess.
I never did address
My love for you.
Yet your kind smile
And gentle eyes
Seemed all along
To realize
That what I really meant to say
Today
Was
That I love you.

Words

We spoke tonight
You and I,
Not high born words,
Simplicity and truth spoke loud.

Your words
A softened plea,
Make my dreams,
Reality.

Those words
Rest gently
Upon
Receptive ears.

They seared
Not just muscle,
And sinew
But coursed through blood.

They travelled
Through veins,
Assaulted arteries,
And settled in my heart.

They filled
That empty cavern,
And told me,
In few words.

That you loved me

A Moment in Time

I lay silently next to you
Bathing in the afterglow
Of love
Above
A jealous moon
Tries boldly to compare
To no avail
A trail of bright stars
Dash across the skies
But my eyes
Can only rest on you
A whisper of your breath
Invades my soul
I lose control
And touch your lustrous hair
Sleep is calling
I'm forestalling
Wanting this moment in time
To last forever.

Coming Home

As a child
I ran wild
Among the valleys of my home.
Bare foot
I trod
The emerald grasses.
The scent
Of morning dew
Grew to be a part of me.
At the foot
Of the valley
Lay my silver stream.
Giggling, Gurgling
Its way
Toward the river Taff.
Black and grey
Trout
Basked in the warmth of a friendly sun.
But adulthood
Stood before me
With all its challenges.
I found love,
I lost love,
Some battles I surrendered.

Then,
One day
You came my way.
And that blue canopy
We call the sky,
Smiled on me.
Now, the empty space
Within my heart
Races to make a home for you.
I can believe
That I'll retrieve
My innocence.
If only
You will come
And tread these fields with me.

In Dreams

Walk with me
Just hold my hand
Together
We can cross this land.

We'll hear the distant Red fox bark
Gaze aloft, and watch the Lark.
Come sit below this ancient Oak
And hear the words that Byron spoke.

We'll gaze at nature's wondrous hue
Which make the bells such perfect blue.
Then dip our fingers in the stream
And close our eyes, perchance to dream.

When stars appear in mighty splendour
And light your form so warm and tender.
With my lips I'll worship you
So you will know my love is true.

On Waking

On waking
I slowly rise
To look down upon you,
Your hair, sleep ruffled
Drifts softly
Across your face.
I am torn
Between touching you
And letting you dream.
Then your eyes flutter
As you stutter
Into wakefulness.
You rest your head
Upon my chest

To gaze at me,
And silently mouth the word,
Coffee.
Reluctantly
I leave our bed
To percolate,
Then wait, for your last sip.
Our first kiss
Is such sweet bliss,
That I need
No second invitation.

Safe Haven

For many years I have drifted
Aimlessly.
Across many seas,
And moored in many harbours.

Some have been too shallow
Others
Provided
No protection from the storms.

Fierce winds have blown me
Far off course
And I have followed the safety
Offered by bogus lighthouses.

I have been hypnotised
By siren song
Whose navigation
Led me onto reefs.

I became resigned
To drifting
And sought
No bearing.

One grey day
While drifting in the fog
Far out to sea
I saw a light.

Without expectation
I followed it
And it led me to a safe haven
It led me to you.

Repaired

Many years ago
When I was young,
Naïve,
My heart was broken,

Shattered,
I collected the pieces
In the hopes of repairing it,
My efforts were in vain.
I, in my turn
Broke other hearts
In my pain,
Again
I tried
To put things right,
But try as I might,
I failed.
So I collected
The many pieces
Of my fractured heart
And started to hide them.
Some in the deepest cracks
Of ancient walls,
Some in crevices
Below the deepest oceans.
It now seems,
That you have, quietly,
Teased these locations
From me,
And recovered them.
You have, patiently,

Stitched the parts together,
Seamlessly.
I awoke one morning
To find my heart,
Reinstalled.
So now, the only thing that I can do
Is trust this new,
Unbroken heart,
To you.

Love's Journey

When love begins
It seems like a race,
The pace
Energetic,
Frenetic,
A train under steam
Rushing headlong
Toward love's sweet song.
As love grows
The pace slows,
Midnight walks
On moonlit sands,
Hands entwined,
Secret smiles

Eat up the miles
As the journey continues.
Then,
As we grow together,
Weather the storms
We need to know more
Before
We truly
Trade hearts.
We start to delve deeper,
Gently,
Below the skin
Searching for the essence
Buried within,
Once discovered
We know
That this is truly,
Where love's journey
Begins

Perspectives

I have often walked these streets
When they seemed dark, stark,
Rain, running down unwelcoming gutters
While a malnourished sun stutters across sullen rooftops.

I have walked by the shore
More for exercise, than pleasure,
The reluctant sea just touching sand,
And rushing off to more promising bays.
I have walked in gardens
Where the blooms seemed to sooner
Turn their heads away,
Than come out to play for the day.
But now.
The streets seem brighter
The shoppers just smile,
While hand-holding lovers
Each other beguile.
It appears, what is more,
That the sea now seems happy
To dance on the sand
And linger a while.
In the gardens, colours flash
Blooms now dash
To become one with the sun,
Fat, striped bees having fun.
It now seems to me
That a new world I see,
And I know that it's true
I am reborn in you.

Should I Know?

I wake each day, and think of you,
My heart rests with you,
The sun rises with you
I think of you.

I walk city streets
I think of you,
I look at the sky
I think of you.

I wait until the day
Is arrested
And I am complete
Though not suggested,
And I think of you.

Know this,
My kiss
Is for you
And only you.

My Thoughts

Come walk with me,
Talk to me,

Hear my thoughts,
I am caught,
Within the web of your love.
The sound of your voice
Ensnares me,
Excites me,
Delights me,
Makes me feel alive.
I need you to know,
I am captured,
Enraptured
By your soul,
The whole of me
Is within you,
It can, but be true
That all I may do,
Is love you.

Priceless

There have been days
When the haze of insecurity
Has threatened to stain
The pristine sheets
Of winter white.
My heart will sink

To depths,
Where I think
Of distant buried pain,
And heartache's
Sad refrain.
Yet you do not fail,
Or rail
Against such ingratitude,
Your words of constancy
Are gifts
To heal all rifts,
And shower me with hope.
Those words
As you,
Are priceless.

The Universe

Remember.............You are everything,

Close your eyes, what do you see?
Nothing....not a cloud, not a bird, not a tree
But you can feel the essence of your being.
Your happiness is the happiness of the world
Your laughter, the only laughter ever heard.
The Sun, the Moon and the stars shine only because of you.

You are not part of the Universe,
You are the Universe,
My Universe.
When you go, the Universe goes with you.
The Sun, the Moon and the stars, all die
And I
Await your return
And the rebirth of the Universe
My Universe,
And the lifting of the veil.

Reality

Aha, so you and I
As much as we reach for the sky
And try, to be fair lovers
Find the ground a little rocky.
I give you all I have,
I try to teach you,
To beseech you,
To tell you that I love you.
You think that I am shallow,
Fallow fields for other furrows,
A tart,
Whose heart is less than yours?
There are no minds

That I could find
That could unwind
The web of love I feel for you.
So, please believe
The webs I weave
Are meant
To capture you.

As Dawn Breaks

As dawn breaks
I awake to find
My mind
Adorned with thoughts of you.

I know that the journey
I must make
To break with the ties of the past,
Is fast approaching.

I need no 747 to fly
For I have wings,
And my heart sings
Songs of you.

As dawn breaks,
My heart aches
To make its way to you,
Today.

There are Days

There are days,
When I seem to decide
I am better off
To reside, in the past,
Though these are fast
Becoming less.
There are days
When I seem not to know
Which way to go,
When I'm lost,
Not counting the cost,
Of such self indulgence.
But throughout these grey days,
You seem to find ways
Of making me breathe,
So I leave the past behind
And find,
My way back to you.

The Fool in Me

It's true
There's always been
A fool in me.
There are times
When I am blinded,
Minded
To let my demons,
Present,
And past,
Have the last say,
As I stray
From the path
You have lit for me.
But I shall
Find my way,
One day,
Away from these illusions
Confusions,
And tread the path of light
Right
To your door.
Please leave it lit,
To guide me.

Today

Take today
For example;
I have missed you
Would have kissed you
Had I had the chance,
But happenstance
Keeps us apart.
I start
To tell you
All the music
That sets my
Heart on fire,
Yet you
Just take
My heart
And start,
Just to make it yours
Of course
I must submit.
It's simple,
I love you,
I shall do
All you want me to.

My Path

I have wandered through
My life
Knowing that the paths taken
Were leading me nowhere,
I knew that loves' lost
Would cost,
But,
Like empires
To dust
I just
Ignored my life.
Eventually,
I sat
Deciding
That grey
Should
Be the day
In which I lived.
Then,
Suddenly,
You
Came into my life,
Taking all the negativity
And turning it

To positivity.
Teaching me
That love
Is not some foolish game.
I listened,
Quietly.
So let me tell you this,
With every kiss
I adore you

These Days

There are days
When I think only of you.
When your mind
Invades mine
And the love
I feel for you
Takes control.
There are other days
When I wait for you
When you decide
That patricide
Is just the death
Of fathers.
I am left

Thinking of you
And the things
That you do.
So, I shall say this
Your kiss
Brings heaven
To my door.

Oceans and Shores

When I think of us
I see you as the ocean
Hidden depths
Intense
Full of mystery
And beauty.
I am the shore
Constant
Silent
Expansive
Forever
Waiting for you.
One day you arrive
Softly
Gently
To kiss

And whisper
Sweet words.
Another day you arrive
Like thunder
Pounding me
With roaring waves
And dragging me to you
In the undertow.
Is it the gravity pull
Of the moon
That raises passions?
This I know
If ever you go
This shoreline will die.

My Favorite Place

I sit mute and wonder,
Lost within my muse,
If this world was ending
Which place would I choose?

The wonder of the Taj Mahal
White marble, cool and clean,
I doubt if I would choose that,
In truth, I've never been.

Or maybe ancient Babylon
The hanging gardens there,
Ingest exotic perfumes
Among the blooms so rare.

The pyramids at Giza
That reach to scrape the sky
I really wouldn't go there
And here's the reason why;

If the world was due to end
I'd know my favourite place,
I'd lay in silence next to you,
And bathe within your grace.

The Essence of You

It comes as no surprise,
That the warmth which shines
From deep within your eyes,
Brings peace to my soul.
Your shy smile,
While lighting rooms,
Brings richness
To my heart.
But, apart from this,

The bliss you bring to me
Endlessly,
Comes from deep inside.
Truth,
Compassion,
Understanding,
Loyalty,
And laughter,
Are also attributes,
Of beauty.
They form the essence
That is truly you.

Everything

These days, everything I do
Takes on new life, because of you.
It seems to me, in every way
I grow in stature, each new day.
The thoughts that now, flow through my mind
Are of a warmer gracious kind.
And though my imperfections show,
Your affections only grow.
So each and every word is true,
I live within the love of you.

Us

I sometimes,
Find things
Hard to say,
Today, is one of them.
I do not give love lightly
I cannot change
Or rearrange,
The way I feel.
If love is real
Then it is eternal.
We must take our chances
Dances, we must make,
Not break the gossamer threads
That connect us.
Trust,
A simple word,
But heard,
Correctly,
It will sustain us,
Through this world,
And beyond,
My love belongs to you,
That is true,
So put your trust in me
And you will see,
That I hold
Your heart close to mine.

Spoiling You

I send my mind
In search, of your mind,
And when we connect,
I find, just what I am looking for.
There is kindness,
Generosity,
Repricocity, (you see, I make up words for you)
Of my feelings for you.
I find hidden corners,
Where pain resides,
Where you hide
Your fears,
Your insecurities,
I find your childhood,
Your teens,
I can touch your favourite jeans.
I want to rest here,
Be blessed here,
Be part of all of you.
In return,
For my tenancy,
I will love you,
I will shower you
With the gifts that I have,

I will sing songs,
Badly,
Recite poetry,
If I find worthy poets,
But,
Most of all,
I will spoil you,
Until you say
No more!
And smile,
While I
Caress you.

Thankyou

As a Cornish dawn breaks
I make my way
Across emerald fields,
To steal a first look
At the sea.
Ancient stones
Alone with their secrets
Ignore me,
Tendrils of early morning mist
Await a lazy sun to set them free.
Young rabbits

Who have ignored their parent's pleas
To be home early
Rush for burrows
In the hope of evading detection.
Rodents, inert,
To avoid
Alert eyes
Of hovering hawks
High above.
My gaze turns
To the fluff littered sky
As I think of you,
And the calmness you bring to my soul,
I wholeheartedly thankyou.

Possibilities

It is late
At night
And though the light
Has dissipated,
I think of you.
Noisy gulls
Mothers and sons,
Fathers and daughters,
Cousins even,

Make their voices heard.
The absurdity of it
Makes me smile.
Yet all the while
I think of you.
Will our voices
Turn into a kiss?
May I expect such bliss?
But I must speak,
Shout loud,
Know this,
Now that I have found you
I shall do nought
Other than surround you
With the love
I have for you,
And leave fate
To possibilities.

My Time

I sit behind my crumbled desk
My quill scratching messages
That no one will ever see
The words tumble
Jumble

In hope I'll set them free.
The ink
Black
But now with gold
As the sun
Shines on it's edges
Tells my story.
Asks,
If glory
Is what I desire.
Within me
Burns desire
For you,
It's true,
I cannot think
Of any day
Or any way
That my love
Shall not come
Your way.
So, think of me
And try to see
That, behind my desk
I need you
To
Rescue me.

WINDSWEPT INSPIRATION

Messages

I've left my footprints in the sand
In hope that you may understand
This trail I leave by emerald sea
To guide you, if you come to me.

I've made a journey to our wood
In hope that you might, if you could
See the words carved in our tree
They'll guide you, if you come to me.

I wrote some words on ancient stone
So you will know you're not alone
These silent words, a heartfelt plea
A prayer that you will come to me.

These messages I've left for you
Come from my heart, and all are true
So here I sit in reverie
And dream that you will come to me.

Gems

To what should I compare thee?
A Diamond?
Hewn from God's earth
Translucent giver of light
Friend of maidens?
An Emerald?
Depths of the oceans
Early cornfields
Mermaids delight
A crown of jealousy?
A Sapphire?
Beauty of the night sky
By Royal command
The view of evening mountains
Or, the sadness within?
A Ruby?
The colour of blood
The bringer of fire and flame
Piercer of the heart
Vision of the setting sun?
None!
For the most beautiful
The most precious
The most desirable
Is thee!

The Eternal Question

Since the world was young
Man has searched for an answer
To the eternal question,
What is love?

Philosophers with mighty tomes
Which fill their homes
Have ruminated, speculated
And gloriously failed.

Romantic poets, such as Keats
With feats of verse
That you and I
Would die to have penned, have failed.

So, why should I
Even try
To win
Where they have failed?

I don't have to ruminate
I do not have to speculate
I do not even have to wait
For someone else's view.

For I have the answer
There is no doubt it's true
The answer to this question
Is that love is YOU.

The Wonder of You

A dark forbidding rock
Climbs high
Above a grey and sullen sea
This lonely shard
Is home to me
My sanctuary.

Sleek grey warships
Silently sail by
All angles and menace
White faces on the bridge
Just stare
And wonder why I'm there.

One morning
Completely without warning
A small sailboat appears
Broken mast
Much torn sails

Its master hails
For help.

I give safe haven
To this stricken craft
And comfort to its
Master.
At first I spoke
In silence.

But then we talked till dawn
And by the morn
The sea was dressed
In different hue
A soft bright blue
With dancing waves.

Dolphins poked there noses
At the sky
And I
The first in many years
Laughed at their frivolity
And held a friendly hand.

Now my jagged rock
Has softened
And
We stroll on golden sand
While I marvel
At the wonder of you.

Walls

As I approach your fortress,
I see the dark forbidding walls,
Towering to scratch the sky,
Stern sentries at every entrance.

I look in silence,
Knowing that these walls,
Protect you from storms,
Pain and heartache cannot permeate.

I set up camp below your towers,
And prepare my vigil,
And draw my quest,
To set you free.

Know this:
I was Joshua's mentor at Jericho,
I aided Ghengis Khan to overcome the Chin,
I instructed Job in the art of patience.

The love I hold for you,
Defies all impediments,
It will forge cracks in these defences,
And let in shards of sunlight.

Tear down your shrouds within,
Replace them with golden tapestries,
Play, at last, sweet music,
To welcome me.

For my love will be your protection,
My love will be your shield,
And your salvation,
You will have no need of walls.

A Candle

Whenever I seem distant
And we seem far apart
Please, my love, look closely
There's the candle in my heart.

Whenever you feel lonely
And I seem far away
Please know the candle in my heart
Will burn both night and day.

When nights are dark and stormy
And rain turns into hail
Look for the light that burns so bright
This candle will not fail.

So when I seem distant
And you feel lost inside
The candle here that burns so bright
Will guide you to my side.

Barriers

I've seen the jagged mountains,
I've heard the roaring seas,
But hear this now, and hear it well,
My love will conquer these.

I'll cross the arid deserts,
Bare foot through burning sands,
I'll find my way past glaciers,
In windswept frozen lands.

There is no forest dark enough,
To bar my way to you,
I need no help from compass,
My love will guide me true.

So, all I ask from you, my love,
Is please wait, and be true,
For I will cross these barriers,
And find my way to you.

Fulfilled

I've wandered ancient forests,
I've sailed forbidden seas,
I've slaked my thirst in mountain streams,
And done most as I please.

I've read the words of poets,
I've deciphered mystic's runes,
I've watched the thoughts of playwrights,
And danced to minstrel's tunes.

I've seen the wonders of this world,
I've held life in my hand,
I've seen the stars light up the sky,
And oceans kiss the sand.

But my black soul was empty,
My heart knew not, love's song,
Until the day the whole world changed,
The day, you came along.

I Ask Only This

I ask only this:
Tonight
Before you sleep
Please kiss
My photograph
And light the fire
That my desire
Requires of you.

I ask only this:
Try to understand
This land
Of dreams
In which I live
Would give
A ransom
For reality.

I ask only this:
While my head spins
And doubt begins
Take my heart
And start
To feed me courage
For I am weak, and seek
Your reassurance.

I ask only this:
Know the love
I feel for you
Is true
And what is more
Know I adore
Everything
That is you.

Just You

How do I find the words
To say how much I love you?

When you are near
My pulses race,
Blood courses through my veins,
To feed the inferno that was once my heart.

Your words blind my senses
Leaving me directionless,
Without a guide,
But heaven bound.

Your touch would reduce me
To hopeless shivers,
My inept vocabulary,
Takes flight upon my breath.

Should you ever deign to kiss me
Or, to brush me with your lips,
Then I would fly in ecstasy,
 Off to dance with stars.

How do I find the words
To say how much I love you?

Only one springs to my mind,
You,

Just.....You.

Know This

When you wake
Know this:
My love for you
Knows no boundaries;
We shall walk
Hand in hand
Across lands
Where mighty cities
Have fallen,
And been reborn.
Where dynasties

Have dissipated
And been replaced
By others,
Only to fade
In their turn.
While our love knows no boundaries.
Stars will be born
And die,
The sun will dim
Day turn to night,
While our love
Lights the universe.
The love songs
We sing
Will bring peace
To all
And though mountains may fall
Our love will grow.
So,
When you wake
Know this:
Our love will last
Past and beyond
Time and space,
As we face
This timeless journey,
Together.

My love's touch

I swim within the depths of you,
The waters warm and calm.
The currents soft, a gentle flow,
Protects me from all harm.

You smile at me, a gentle breeze,
Calms my troubled soul.
One gaze from your soft loving eyes,
Makes what was broken whole.

One touch from slender fingers,
Can set my heart on fire.
One kiss from tender perfumed lips
Creates such deep desire.

Winter holds no power,
To chill the love that burns.
Your voice, a message on the wind
Will stay till spring returns.

I know this love, which burns so bright
Will never pass away.
So I sit warm, and so content
Touched by your love, today.

Never To Wake

When you look at me
I feel I'm made of glass
That you see transparency
The flaws in me
But no
You just smile enigmatically.

When you touch me
My nerve endings
Come alive
I strive to appear cool
But, like a fool
I tremble.

When I speak
My foolish words
You seem rapt
Captivated
As if I sing
A melody.

Oftentimes I feel
As if there is no reality
And I live
Within a dream
My only wish
Is never to wake.

Darkness to Light

You've turned the darkness into light,
Brought the day, and banished night.
You've blown away the clouds and rain,
And let the sunshine in again.
The winter now has turned to spring,
I even hear the children sing.
The joy I feel, in every way,
Increases with each passing day.
One touch, one word, one loving gaze,
Can set my frozen soul ablaze.
My heart is yours, to have and hold,
From now until the world grows old.

If Only

I think of all the things I've said,
Then thought of different things, instead.
I think of all that I have done,
When moons were cheese, and life was fun.

But now I sit, and realize,
I lost the one and only prize.
The one who gave me butterflies,
Whose depth was shown, within her eyes.

So, now I sit, in loneliness,
Cold, without her warm caress.
Wondering, what might have been,
If only, I might just have seen........

My Gift

I had thought
To give you
The Moon and the Stars
But they are far from my reach,
Their loss
Would mean
The death of Poets
And Wolves.
I had considered
The autumn breeze,
But how would the trees
Shed amber leaves
And prepare for winter's trials?
I thought of priceless gems,
But they are cold
And would seem as glass
Compared to your beauty.
I thought of my words,
Though they are a jumble

That tumble
From a disordered mind.
So,
Just for a start
I shall give you
My heart
And ask
That you treasure it
As I treasure you.

The Beauty of Silence

We sit
Quietly,
Close to the light
Of a bright log fire,
Reading,
Not needing
Conversation.
Our thoughts coalesce,
Just one heart
We possess.
I rest my book
And look up
At your smile,
Then I know

In a while
Concentration will break,
For I'm eager to take
Your sweet form
In my arms
Resting all through the night
Among wondrous charms.

Sounds

I have lived many lifetimes,
And heard much,
Such as the sounds;
Of a gentle breeze,
Kissing leaves
On an Autumn afternoon.
Of politicians, telling lies
Unsurprisingly.
Of morning birds'
Sweet summer songs.
Of priests, promising salvation,
When they have no faith.
Of new life
In springtime.
Of gunfire,
In dark streets.

Of the silence of snow
In winter.
But the sweetest sounds
I have ever heard,
Are the beats of your heart,
The sweet bells of your laughter,
The melody of your voice
Each one refreshes my soul
Breathing new life through my veins.
So, the sound I now utter,
Is, Thankyou.

Resurrection

I have spent many days, lonely
Only waiting for the end
I have intended
To speak to no one.
I've wandered city streets,
Replete
In my self indulgence.
Ignoring all around me,
The gifts that truly surround me.
Then,
From out of the blue
Came you,

Calming voice,
Offering choice,
And telling me to leave my demons behind.
How kind
Are you,
I know
Your words are true,
And I feel
Resurrected.

In Wonder

There are many wonders
In this world of ours,
The best
Stand the test of time.
The sun shines
Giving light to our lives,
The moon casts a silver sheen
On our dreams.
The seasons come, and go,
Each providing
A different glow.
The oceans, and the seas,
Are pleased
To give muse

To sleep deprived poets.
Men, and women,
Have built monuments
Which proudly stand
For generations.
But,
If I had the chance,
Not one of these wonders
Would warrant a glance,
For I would rest true,
In the wonder
Of you.

Because of You

For a very long time
I lived in the dark,
Stark
Were the thoughts
That wandered my mind,
I kind of got used to them.
Grey days,
Black nights,
Why fight?
I might as well celebrate
The status quo,

Go with the flow,
At least that way I knew where to go.
Yes,
The sun still shone,
But the light
In my eyes,
Had long gone.
Then out of the blue
You appeared,
Sending light,
Forcing me to fight
The darkness within,
Making me believe
I could win.
And I know that it's true
That I am what I am,
Because of you.

Fear Not

Fear not
For I have got
Much love in store,
For all the years to come.
Forget the past,
The love we have

Will last,
Past this life, and beyond.
Just hold my hand
And I will help you
Dance upon the moon,
Much sooner than you think.
And as each day
May close,
Do not suppose
That I shall let you sleep
Without my heart to safely keep
Within your love filled soul.

Images

I sit at my desk
Surrounded by images,
Memories
Of bygone days
When sunshine's rays
Stabbed at the gloom.
Tendrils of tunes
Whisper through my brain
And settle like rain
On a soft summer's day.
With shaking hand
I scribble on card,

As a guard
To protect these treasures
Which I toss to the skies
In the hope that your eyes
Will rest upon them
And smile.

Contrasts

I've seen things in black and white
Grey just seems to not look right.
I've viewed things as right or wrong
No middle ground within my song.

Things are either cold, or hot
I don't like slightly warm, a lot.
I've never sat upon the fence
And vague opinions make no sense.

But ever since you came along
I seem to sing a different song.
Now I'm never really sure
What my opinions were before.

It's as if I'm back in school
Behaving like a childish fool.
Now I'm confused, I know that's true
And all of it, because of you.

I hope it never changes!

I have wondered

There have been times
That I have wondered,
Conjectured,
Thought about you,
And tried to decide
If I truly loved you.
But then,
Your eyes
Surprised me
And I knew
This love was true.
Stay with me,
Play with me,
And let me stay with you.

From Light to Darkness

There are days
When my darkness
Blocks out all light,
Even the brightness
You have the kindness
To shine on me.
I worry,
Hurry to make judgements

That I know are unfair,
Love scares me,
I am not prepared
Scared,
That it is too late
And fate
Has stolen this chance.
But,
Know this
If I miss this chance
There will
Never be another.
Yet I
Am such a poor
Lover.
I have treated
Fate
Badly, and sadly
It wants a reward.

Just Another Day

I walk the streets,
My feet,
Seem heavy, at first,
But then I think of you

And, suddenly,
I walk on air
Without so much
As the smallest of cares.
I look at passers by
And wonder why
They are not at work?
Do they shirk?
Or are they like me,
Deep in reverie?
The shop windows
Hold no attraction,
I am already deep in distraction,
All I do
Is think of you,
And wonder what you do.
As I wander, on my way
I suddenly realise,
Today,
Is no different,
To all
My days.

Thankyou

As a Cornish dawn breaks
I make my way
Across emerald fields,
To steal a first look
At the sea.
Ancient stones
Alone with their secrets
Ignore me,
Tendrils of early morning mist
Await a lazy sun to set them free.
Young rabbits
Who have ignored their parent's pleas
To be home early
Rush for burrows
In the hope of evading detection.
Rodents, inert,
To a avoid
Alert eyes
Of hovering hawks
High above.
My gaze turns
To the fluff littered sky
As I think of you,
And the calmness you bring to my soul,
I wholeheartedly thankyou.

Your Presence

During these expectant days of spring,
Your voice comes to me
As if upon a breeze,
Your gaze rests upon me
Through golden swaying daffodils,
Your touch upon my skin
Like the breath of butterflies.
During these clear expectant nights of spring
I hear your voice
Melodic, like soft silver bells,
I feel your gaze
Through the haze
Of a newly minted moon,
You touch me
With stardust.
Even when you go away
Each day
I still feel your presence.

WINDSWEPT REFLECTIONS

Wishes

Every day, when I awake,
I think of you.
Every night, before I sleep,
I think of you.
The dreams I have,
Encompass you.
The best of me,
Resides in you.
The sun now shines
Within your eyes,
And darkness
Wraps its cloak, and flies.
If I could wish,
For just one thing,
And make, the love,
In your heart sing,
I would!!
So, I shall dream
My dreams of you,
And wish, one day,
They may come true

A Spell

I lived a life of grey
Each day
As many do,
The occasional shaft of light
Broke through.
Then I saw you,
I wanted to talk
But baulked at the thought.
You spoke to me
And suddenly:
I was connected,
Dissected,
Resurrected,
Infected,
You cast a spell on me,
From which
I beg,
No release.

Visions

Each morning, when I awake,
My thoughts turn to you.
I think of you brushing your hair,
And the sleep from your eyes.

I imagine you dressing,
Checking your perfection,
One last time,
In a grateful mirror.
I see you at your work,
Granting soft smiles,
To lucky recipients,
Spreading light in dark corners.
I watch you shopping,
For simple items,
Leaving warmth,
In the chill cabinets.
In the evening, with a book,
Music swirling, caressing you.
Each night before I sleep,
My thoughts turn to you.

Tonight

Tonight, I sit and think of you,
I have known you before,
I remain unsure
Of where
Or when.
But then, again
Should I question this?

Owain Glyn

I remember
Our first kiss
And the bliss
It brought
Me
Caught
Within your web.
We rode across
The silent steppes
Hair blown
Now adept
At love.
Deserts
Saw us
And we knew
If love
Was true
Then it was us.
As cities fall
All I say is this,
Grasp my hand
And understand
I love you.

Time

I sit solitary, in pensive muse
Arms wrapped tight
Around my knees
Amid these, the highest peaks.

As I gaze down
Through frozen mist
That kissed these ancient rocks
I think of time.

My knowing fingers
Scrape the sky
And I
Think now of you.

A third of life
We spend asleep
And keep that time
For muddled dreams.

The second third
We use to earn
To learn, the skills
That are necessity.

The final third
Is ours to play
And find our way
Through love.

But when, my love
We disagree
We waste this time
So foolishly.

Time that bears a heavy cost
Time that is forever lost
Time that was for you and me
Time that now will never be.

Time flies; let us rest upon its wings.

Things Left Undone

There are times
When my mind
Has a mind of its own.
It decides by itself
What it wishes to do,
And when it decides
To think only of you,

The things I should do
Are left undone.
Shoes are left unpolished,
Letters I might write
Are left unwritten,
Unposted.
Cups and coffee dregs
Lay unwashed, languishing,
In an overcrowded sink
I think
Only thoughts of you
Not the things that I should do.
I wonder if you see the same sky
As I do,
I forget to shave,
A grave state of affairs,
As I sit on the stairs
Wondering
If I meant to go up,
Or whether I have just come down.
I don't mind
My mind
Having a mind of its own
If it's thinking of you
Instead
Of the things I should do.

The Night

The sun
Gives a final blink
As it sinks
To rest
Deep in the west.
Sister moon
Will soon
Sit high
In velvet sky
Dressed in stars.
Shops will light
In hope
That passers by
Just might
Stop one last time, and buy.
Star crossed lovers
Hide in dark alleys
To steal a kiss,
And hope to miss
Prying eyes.

The Beauty Within

I sit quietly in the dark hours
As I am wont to do
And think of you.
My mind searches for comparisons;
I see frozen oceans
And the stark blue white
Icebergs,
Beautiful statues carved not by man
But by nature.
I reflect that what I see
Is not the whole,
As they drift in tranquillity
Their true beauty
Rests beneath the sea
Where rests their true reality.
My mind flies in reverie
To sculptured deserts
Where ancient pyramids stand
Proudly in the sand.
Magnificent
Against the sky
I know
That their true treasures
Lie below

With sleeping Kings.
As it is with you:
The beauty of your form
Your silk translucent skin
Wherein hides the true beauty.
All your fears,
Your unshed tears
Your burning passion
And your warmth
Are buried deep within your soul
But they make up
The whole of you.
So give them wings
And let them fly,
So I may find the space
To take my place
And rest my heart in yours.

Siren's Song

The song of the siren
Courses through my veins
Calling me to the depths
With promises of ecstasy
But the power of my love
Holds me firm.

I think of you
And why you consume me,
Is it the softness of your skin?
As my fingers wander
Among the hills and valleys
Of your sweet form.

Or is it the wonder
Of your eyes
Which seem to realise
All that is good in me?
Or the way you fan the fire
Of my desire?

But deep inside I know,
It is far more than this
The kiss of your essence
Is what keeps me strong
As I ignore
The siren song.

Silent Night

I stand and look out
Over the bay.
The night is still
And silent.
The waves slip silently
To shore.
The town is quiet.
Children in warm beds
Hug teddy bears
While sucking thumbs.
Down stairs
Parents worry about bills.
Husbands hope their wives
Will not have headaches
Tonight.
Barmen wash the last
Of the dirty glasses
And dream
Of jobs
As computer programmers.
Lonely Policemen
Walk
Bored and silent
The only crime on their minds

Involves beautiful television
Weather girls.
The butcher
Looks at his receipts
And wonders
If he should
Fiddle his VAT
To make ends meet.
All I can think of
Is you.

In my Mind's Eye

In my mind's eye
I see the world
Through differing hues.

The pastel shades
Of spring
Sing of renewal.

The vibrant yellows,
The cerulean blues
Of summer.

The reds and golds
Of autumn days
Amaze me.

The crisp cold nights
Of winter white
Delight in their own way.

But to be true,
In my mind's eye,
I wish to see the world with you.

Understanding

I wish that I could understand,
I'd follow footsteps, in the sand.
My essence I would give to you,
And I would beg you to be true.

I know the things that I've done wrong,
Will never make the perfect song.
But, if anything is true,
It starts within my love for you.

The tide cannot achieve the shore,
The sun can't shine, and what is more,

That everything I have will rest,
In you, when we have just caressed.

Give to me this final chance,
So I may just this once, perchance,
Show you the love I have to give,
So we, in harmony, might live.

By Candlelight

When I think of you
Which is often
I like to think of you
In candlelight.
Gazing at your sleeping form
I watch the light
Dance upon your skin
Creating soft moving shadows.
I am tempted to touch you
But you look fragile
In sleep.
But I know
You have the inner strength
And grace
Of a lioness.
There are times
When I think we have just met

And others
Where I have known you
For a lifetime
Many lifetimes past
And many lifetimes
To come.
Death now holds
No dominion over me.

Grey Days

There are days
When I bask in the haze of the sun
Having fun
Weaving webs, of words.

They are not meant
To break hearts
Or start wars
But once writ, they can't be undone.

Then, some days
Are grey,
They reflect no sun,
And the fun of weaving flies away.

So, maybe some days
It might be best
To rest my pen
And think again.

But you should know this;
That when my pen
Kisses paper again
It is truly for you.

How Do You Do That?

When I awake, before my eyes are yet open,
I see pictures
Of Dante's nine levels,
The unfaithful, choking on the sour worms of deceit,
Liars, upside down in boiling oil,
The slothful hauling rocks
Two-headed demons feasting on thieves
Souls screaming, as they cascade into the cacophony below.
Suddenly,
A picture of you comes to me
The sun assaults my curtains
The sweet perfume of summer blooms
Fills the room
Morning birds

Owain Glyn

Sing morning songs
And all is well with the world.
How do you do that?

TRUST

I awoke, sleep ruffled,
I looked across at a pillow,
Sometimes, shared.
I saw a creature, reclining there,
I recognized it,
Trust.

It gazed at me,
With soulful eyes.
Questioning eyes.
Are you about to give me away?
Have you found a home for me?
Trust.

I reflected,
If I give you away,
Today
Into other hands.
Will you be nurtured?
Protected?

Or will your fragility
Be exploited?
Laid bare, for all to see,
My vulnerability?
If I entrust my trust to you,
What will you do?

I think I know the answer
So, I give this precious gift freely.

Questions

I sit, often, late at night
And ponder,
I wonder
Where life will take us
You and I,
I try to imagine
How things will be,
If we
Ever become one.
It is not
That I regret
My past
Though, it fast
Becomes whispers
In the cacophony

Of my life.
Just think, my love,
We can drink
Each other's lives,
And become intoxicated
Renovated
Re-evaluated,
And sated
With the sight
Of each other.
We can learn,
Earn
Each other's love
Then rest,
In the best
Of each other.
So when I sit,
Late
At night
And ponder,
Wonder
Where life will take us,
Know this:
I think of us.

Lightning

My life, like many others,
Was a catalogue
Of missed opportunities
And poor decisions.
I had built empires,
Only to see them fall.
My castles,
Crumble to dust.
I felt confined, resigned
To spend my days
Sheltered from confusion,
Free from life's illusion.
Then lightening blew the dark apart,
Seared my heart,
Lit up my soul,
And made me whole, again.
Now I believe
In Suns and Moons
And lover's tunes,
All because of you.

Morning Thoughts

I wake to the sound of raucous gulls
Each trying to be louder than the sea,
Succeeding, gleefully.
I lay quietly
With my thoughts,
Drifting softly.

Other than a first love,
Tossed aside
Through naiveté,
I have tried to live
A quiet life,
Avoiding strife.

Taken middle roads,
Stick to mundane,
Less pain, I thought,
You caught my eye
And I
Was lost in you.

True, I thought it would not last,
A fast escape by you.
Yet, if truth were told,
If I played bold,
I might keep hold
Of you.

So now,
My morning thoughts
Are all of you,
And the things I must do
To stay true
This time.

Silence

I sit here
Quietly
And wait for you,
My tongue
And the words
That slip from it
Are
Yours,
Could it be?
I love you?

Inside My Mind

Recently,
Increasingly,
I find my mind
Just makes its way
To you.
It needs no help
From me,
Seemingly.
I appear
To bathe endlessly,
Within your eyes
Before I even realize
There is a world outside.
I do not care,
No wish, have I
To share my time with you.
Could it be?
That the touch
Of your hand
Will bring me
To reality
Eventually?
I hope not
For I have got
All I need in you.

Rainbow

I sit on the bay,
With my head in my hands,
And I watch as the rain
Gently washes the sands.

If I had a heart
I would look deep inside,
And search for the love,
Which I always denied.

Above soar the gulls,
Grey squadrons in flight
As I lift tired eyes,
In search of the night.

Instead, there's a rainbow,
Which graces the sky,
Spreading light all around,
As the rain starts to die.

I do not think of treasure,
Or of cauldrons of gold.
I just think of you,
As the years now unfold.

Can you see this rainbow?
Which graces the sky?
As the soft, gentle rain
Joins the tears that I cry.

Words Spoken and Unspoken

There was a time
When my words
Reached soft fluffy clouds,
I was happy.
Now,
It seems these words
Return,
Misunderstood,
And only good
As rain,
For some lost parade.
Should I be more kind?
I mind not
That you should think so.
And if it means
That I must rearrange
Myself,
So be it.
Have I made mistakes?

Oh yes!!
I guess you know that well.
Though when my words,
Absurd, or not,
Scatter upon such very barren ground,
The sound,
Destroys me.
Take the love
I have for you,
And spread it lightly
On those words,
Absurd, or not.

Me the Poet

Where, truly, is the poet in me?
I try to make you see,
The words
I drag from the depths of my soul,
I think, that somehow,
They will make me whole,
And we can travel
This road,
Together.
But, it seems,
My dreams,

Are littered with mistakes,
And I take
The wrong road,
Yet again.
But you remain,
Like a beacon
That shines,
Through the rain,
Providing direction,
On reflection,
I shall listen,
And make it my mission,
To find my way,
To you.

In Days Past

In days long gone
The song I sang
Was different to today,
In a way,
I was different too,
That is surely true.

I lived life fast
And cast my net
Wherever

Prey was ample,
For example,
I took what I could catch, no match for me.

As the years have past,
I live with my sins,
My demons.
I have killed,
And was, to a degree,
Thrilled.

But now,
I sit in darkened rooms,
And try to contemplate
My fate.
But fearful I am not,
For suddenly I have got, you.

You came to me from nowhere,
You seemed
Not to care
About my chequered past,
And now, at last,
You bring me peace.

How can I be
But thankful.

As Each Day Passes

As each day passes
I think of you,
Trying to visualise
The things that you do.

We talk, sometimes,
But, we baulk,
Never talk,
Of the distance between us.

I think it is clear,
We both fear
That the future
We need, may be dear.

Worry not,
For I have got
A plan, and if I can,
I shall bring it home.

Trust in me,
Believe in me,
Rest your hopes in me,
And we shall see.

I shall try
Why should I not?
To bring to you
A love, so true.

The Words That I Write

In the depths of the night,
Winds howling from the sea,
I drift lazily,
Thinking of the words I write
For you.
They come from deep
Within my soul,
Sometimes whole phrases,
At other times,
Single words,
Grace,
Patience,
Loyalty,
Warmth,
Are but a few.
There are many I discard,
I find it hard
Sometimes,
The lines are blurred,

With words that don't do justice
To the way I truly feel.
So,
This night,
While I'm awake,
I'll try to find the words
That make you understand
How much
I truly love you.

My Thoughts

Come walk with me,
Talk to me,
Hear my thoughts,
I am caught,
Within the web of your love.
The sound of your voice
Ensnares me,
Excites me,
Delights me,
Makes me feel alive.
I need you to know,
I am captured,
Enraptured
By your soul,

The whole of me
Is within you,
It can, but be true
That all I may do,

Is love you.

As Day Breaks

As day breaks
And I wake,
I hear morning birds
Sing morning songs,
Throngs pass,
Setting the new day's
Hour glass
To meet their needs.
Bakers bake,
Paper boys take
Their bicycles
To spread the news,
Poet's muse
Takes hold,
In the hope
That words of gold
Will leave their pens.
Wives send husbands

On their way
For some,
A time for lovers play.
For me,
The day takes on a rainbow hue
As I close my eyes
Once more,
And think of you.

Where are you Now

I awake, I think of you
I think of your smile
And smile within your eyes
I remember your caress.

Where are you now?
Do your eyes still smile?
Is your touch as soft?
Does your voice still open souls?

If the world still has hope
I will search for you,
If destiny is true
I will find you..

And love you.

Colours

Recently,
Some days
Have turned to black,
I seemed
To be back
To my old ways,
Where grey was the colour of the day.
Persistent rain
Beat soulful tunes
On grimy window panes,
Then,
I caught the light of your smile,
And in a short while
The drab hues
Turned to blues,
As the sun broke through.
So,
I need you
To know,
It is only you
Who can do this,
And I gently kiss
The very thought of you.

WINDSWEPT SEASONS

Spring in Nigh

The dark grey days
Now pass away,
Chased on the wing
By impending spring.
Winter's hills
Welcome daffodils,
And Jack Frost flees
The waking trees.
My heart wakes too
Because of you,
My soul can sing
Of this new spring.
For this awakening,
This dawn,
This season new,
All rests, in you.

A Taste of Spring

Spring has arrived, softly,
No fanfare,
No peal of bells,
The only herald, a change in the air.

I lift my feet and point them,
Eagerly,
Toward the Cornish lanes
That lead to gorse dressed moors.

Verges boast a host
Of Wordsworth's daffodils,
And yes, today,
They truly dance and sway.

Young hares, and rodents, jump, and run
As if today
Were made
For fun.

It seems to me,
That now
I view life differently,
And all because of you

Seasons

As a lazy spring sun
Climbs from its bed
To shed warming rays
That turn dew to gems,
I will come to you.

As a soft summer breeze
Steals through your window,
To ruffle your hair,
And dare, to kiss the sleep from your eyes
I will come to you.

When autumn leaves
Dressed in red and gold,
Loosen their hold
To chase squirrels to bed,
I will come to you.

When cold winter nights
Lose the light
And frost adorns
White painted morns,
I will come to you.

For as the seasons change
To rearrange
Your world,
I will be your constant,
I will come to you.

A Soft Summers Day

We sit by the stream
On this soft summers day
Entranced by the dance
As the Dragonflies play.

A waggle tailed Moorhen
Leads young to the nest
While the arrogant Swan
Knows she's looking her best.

In the meadow the mad Hare
Continues the chase
As the spider weaves webs
That the sun turns to lace.

Overhead soft white pillows
Cross pastel blue skies
And I gaze with pure joy
As I see skylarks rise.

I look at you sleeping, a smile on my face
And I thank Mother Nature for sharing this place.
The silver stream gurgles on its merry way.
As I glory in you, and a soft summers day.

Winter with You

As the first breath of spring
Touches the meadows
And the larks take to wing
My thoughts are with you.

When the summer sun
Warms the cool sea
And industrious bees make honey
My thoughts are with you.

When autumn dresses the trees
In glorious gold
And fairy queens hold court
My thoughts are with you.

But when winter paints the soft earth white
And nights are clear and star filled
I shall lay by a blazing fire with you
And know that dreams may yet come true.

The Colours of Autumn

I used to sit in my room
And stare out over the ocean
Even at the zenith
Of summer
The ocean was grey
Most days.

Trees
In summer dresses
Looked drab
And disinterested
Infested
With lethargy.

Then, one day
You came to me
And softly whispered
Of another life
With the promise
Of a kiss.

Now autumn shows me
A different hue
The ocean is blue
And the trees
Dance
In garments of gold.

I think I may
Decorate my room
In red and gold
To dispel the gloom
And celebrate
You.

The Storm

We sit quietly
Within these granite walls.
Outside
The storm rages.
Howling wind
Races across the bay
Forcing resistant waves
High above
The stoic sea wall.
Stair rod rain

Chases those foolish enough
To cater to canine whims.
We gaze at a lively fire
Within a happy hearth.
The dancing flames
Cast mischievous shadows
On patient walls.
My fingers
Softly insinuate themselves
In yours
And your warmth
Gently heats my blood.
I gaze into smiling eyes

And I know
That very soon
We will create
A storm
That will be stronger
And last longer
Than the one
That rages
Outside
These granite walls.

No Dominion

Winter forces its icy grip
Across the land
The north wind rushes in
Buffeting cities, towns, and villages alike.
It quarrels with itself
As it tears apart
To race down streets
Shaking casements
Behind which lovers
Grow closer.
It picks up crispy leaves
And sneaks through eaves
To wake cosy rodents.
In its mad rush
To realign
Its malign purpose
It leaves a legacy
Behind.
The beauty
Of intricately
Frosted window panes
Which
On the dawn
Will be despoiled

By sleep warmed children's palms
In the search of snow.
It leaves the towns and cities
To dash across the fields
Turning village ponds
To ice rinks
Where placid ducks
May dance.
But in its wild malevolence
I see that
It has no dominion
Over me.
For I am free
You taught me
That spring
With all its magic
Dances merrily behind
And I will find
That birds have found
Their voices.
A symphony
Will greet me
With the coming dawn
And daffodils
Adorn
The waking fields.

So, tonight
It is fair to say
I sleep without a care
Because of you
And winter
Has no dominion
Over me.

Why

I gaze at the beauty that surrounds me.
Trees in glorious summer dress,
Spreading wings,
As canopies for reclining lovers.

Flowers, pregnant in full bloom,
Awaiting buzzing lovers,
To fulfil their purpose,
And to savour sweet perfume.

An emerald sea, so gently,
Caressing soft white sands,
Drifting over toes,
Of lovers holding hands.

Owain Glyn

Snow white cumulus,
Drift slowly,
Lazily,
Across a cerulean sky.

And,
I ask myself,
Why?

Why am I still here, and not at home?

The home where I belong,
Where all such beauty resides,
Within you,
Why?

These October days

These late October days,
Remnants of the haze of summer,
Slate grey seas and skies
Collide.
Clocks go ticking, tocking,
Backward,
In search of light,
That we might look
Forward.

In multi hued parks,
Squirrels
Make last minute shopping trips
Stocking cupboards,
To last until spring.
In the high street
Shops are in their underwear,
Awaiting Christmas dresses,
And credit cards,
That have dieted.
No more morning songs
From morning birds,
They have used the time,
To head for warmer climes.
But,
No longer
Do I allow
These grey days to phase me.
For the light you shine
Upon my soul,
Helps me realise,
This, is just one season,
And reason dictates
That it will pass,
Whereas,
You will stay
Forever.

WINDSWEPT HUMOR

What Would You Do?

What would you do
If I turned up on your doorstep
At two in the morning
Dressed only in my violin?
You know,
The one without a bow
That I play in the metro
Tunnel,
Surrounded by funnel web spiders.
I don't stay,
Because they say
It's illegal,
And anyway
I can't play.
This is nonsense
Of course,
Just like
The pantomime horse
On my bedroom wall.
All I really want to say,
Is what would you do
If I turned up on your doorstep
At two in the morning
Dressed only in my violin?
Would you send me away?
Because I can't play?

My Christmas Present

I've bought this large red fur lined suit
And knee length boots of black
I bought them in a clearance sale,
So I can't take them back.

I've rustled up some reindeer,
And stolen next door's sleigh,
I'll hook the two together,
Then I'll get on my way.

I can't afford a satnav,
I'll manage with a map,
It seems to stop at Dover,
So the thing is pretty crap!

I'll make my way up to the sky,
And gather you some stars,
I'll wrap them up in moondust,
And pretend they came from Mars.

Do you have a chimney?
One that I will fit?
I really do not wish to look,
A red, fat, stupid git!

But know I'll make all efforts,
To be with you Christmas day,
Please try to be patient,
In case I lose my way!

The Man in the Moon

If tonight
You deign to gaze
At the heavens
You will see the wonder
Of a crescent moon.
If you look even closer
You will see me
Perched on the very tip
(I hope I don't slip!)
I hold a fishing rod
With a hook that is bent,
It is my intent
To catch a falling star,
Which I'll place in a jar
On my window sill
Until
The day that you pass
And see through the glass
The light that will shine

To say
Please be mine.
Now the man-in-moon
Is wearing a frown
I think that he's figured
I don't have a clue
How the hell to get down!!

Oh! The things I do for love!!

There Is No Cure

My friends say lately, that I've changed,
Some think, I've become deranged.
Others think I'm simply strange,
They cannot understand this change.

They catch me staring into space,
As if my mind has fled this place.
They think I've lost all interest,
And say, a doctor might be best.

All I really see is you,
There's nothing else I want to do.
I'm living life within this dream,
I want no other, it would seem.

My friends say there must be a cure,
As for me, I'm not so sure.
So, my love, I ask you, please,
Have you contracted this disease?

Assistance.

I have been thinking that I might offer God some assistance.
You see, I am a management consultant.
I can prepare cashflow forecasts:
I can write and construct budgets:
I can read a balance sheet:
I can prepare a business plan:
I am skilled in Logistics:
I understand Human Resources Management.

But my real specialism
Is in stock management,
We call it inventory management.
The reason I mention this
Is because he appears to have lost an Angel,
I know this,
Because I have found her
And I shall keep her as my fee.

Another Chance?

I walk the short mile to town
Head down,
A permanent frown
On my face.
Questions weave and dance
Through my mind,
Do I deserve this chance?
Am I worthy?
I seem to have lived
Most of my life,
Grey suited,
Grey booted,
Plain, and mundane.
Yet, I know you don't see things this way,
Today,
Or any other day.
Angry car horns blare
I don't care,
I can't even remember now,
Why I came to town,
So, I turn around
To walk the short mile home,
With a smile.
I'll come to town
Another day,
If I can remember
What I came for.

ABOUT THE AUTHOR

Owain is a Welsh exile, currently living on the wild coast of Cornwall, UK, a land of legend, from King Arthur, and Merlin, to mermaids, pirates, and smugglers.

 Inspired by his surroundings and his love of words he writes on a wide range of subjects, from romance, to humour, politics, dark spiritual matters, and children's poetry. His intense interest in all aspects of the human condition, stimulate him to write on in a style which he hopes is accessible to all.

Owain Glyn is a popular poet on Wattpad, (https://www.wattpad.com/home) a social network of people who love words, where his poetry has attracted more than 12,000 loyal fans.

His collection of poems, Windswept, has achieved over 2,000,000 reads.

You can read more about Owain Glyn at his web site – coming soon at www.owainglynpoet.com

WANT A SIGNED COPY FROM OWAIN GLYN?

Owain Glyn has commissioned a limited number of signed, personalized copies of Windswept for his fans.
Order yours at the Outer Banks Publishing Group Bookstore at http://bit.ly/1jwnVVY